Quick-to-Stitch
Prayer Shawls

Annie's Attic®

What is a Prayer Shawl?

For those of us who love to crochet, nothing is as soothing as the gentle touch of soft and silky yarn as it glides through our fingers; nothing is as calming as the smooth, steady movements of our hook as we deftly fashion our beautiful creations. As our hands move quickly and surely over our work, the repetitive motion of crocheting the familiar stitches allows our minds to relax and drift. As we work, our thoughts often turn to friends and loved ones, especially if we are creating a gift for them. If we feel worried or concerned, it is natural that we would softly breathe a prayer, asking for God's blessings for them as we stitch along:

> Father, please let Kara's baby be healthy and strong.
>
> • • •
>
> Dear God, please give Martha the courage and strength she needs to face the coming months.
>
> • • •
>
> Oh Lord, bless my loved one with your healing touch!
>
> • • •

These prayers and blessings become as much a part of the fabric of the crocheted item as the yarn itself. The finished items become physical expressions of our prayers, a reminder of our love and God's blessings. These items are gifts like no other gifts—gifts of hope, of comfort, of peace and of love.

We crocheters have been blessed because we can use the talent God has given us to create a special wrap or afghan, called a Prayer Shawl, for those we care about and love. Just wrapping up in one of these beautiful shawls will remind the recipient of your prayers and the love with which it was created.

Creating a Prayer Shawl

Select a yarn that is soft and pleasing to the touch. Prayer Shawls are meant to be snuggled in. Choose a color that is soothing or that is a favorite of the recipient. Make sure the yarn you choose is machine washable and dryable.

Before beginning to stitch, think about the recipients, about your love and concern for them. Give thanks that you have been blessed with the talent to create a gift that will bring the person comfort and joy!

Dear God,

Thank You for blessing me with the ability to crochet! Thank You for the joy, the peace and the many blessings it brings into my life. This ability is a gift which has brought me countless hours of pleasure and enjoyment.

Now Father, I return this gift to You. Please use this talent to serve Your purpose in the world. I pray that You will bless each item I crochet and fill these items with Your spirit, so that they may become physical expressions of Your love. May they radiate peace, goodwill, comfort and, most of all, Your divine love to the recipients.

Amen.

• • •

Now, think of the person for whom you are creating the Prayer Shawl. Let the love you feel for her or him fill your heart and mind; then offer up a prayer for that person. *(See prayers listed with each item)*. As you crochet the Shawl, continue to pray and ask for God's blessings for that person with each stitch:

Bless you, Papa, with God's healing love.

• • •

Lord, bless this marriage with your wisdom and love.

• • •

May the peace of God comfort you, Sue.

• • •

When you have completed the item, ask for God's blessings on it before giving it to the recipient:

Heavenly Father,

Thank You for helping me complete this Shawl for my loved one. I pray that it will bring comfort, joy and peace to Mary in good times, and in those especially difficult times when she needs to feel Your touch. May it be a constant reminder that You are always with her, and that she is loved and cared for. May it warm not only her body, but her heart as well. In Jesus' name I pray, Amen.

• • •

You may want to create a tag to hang on the Shawl, explaining why and how it was made:

I made this Prayer- Shawl especially for you,_____. With each stitch, I prayed that God would bless you with His loving touch. May this shawl always be a reminder of how much I care about you and how much you are loved!

• • •

Present the finished Prayer Shawl to the recipient with a hug and your sincere best wishes for the person's health and happiness!

Crocheting a Prayer Shawl is a special act of love, a creative method of prayer. The time spent in prayer, combined with the restful, physical act of crocheting can have a soothing, meditative effect. You may be surprised to find that making a Prayer Shawl blesses not only the person who receives it, but you, the crocheter, as well!

Scripture Readings

For Peace

Philippians 4:7

And the peace of God, which transcends all understanding, will guard your hearts and your minds in Christ Jesus.

For Healing

Jeremiah 33:6

Nevertheless, I will bring health and healing to it; I will heal my people and will let them enjoy abundant peace and security.

For Love

Genesis 2:24

For this reason a man will leave his father and mother and be united to his wife, and they will become one flesh.

For Life

Psalms 71:6

From birth I have relied on you; you brought me forth from my mother's womb. I will ever praise you.

For a Loved One

John 13:34

"A new command I give you: Love one another. As I have loved you, so you must love one another."

For a Friend

3 John 1:2

Dear friend, I pray that you may enjoy good health and that all may go well with you, even as your soul is getting along well.

For Hope

Psalms 33:20

We wait in hope for the LORD; he is our help and our shield.

For Comfort

Psalms 23:4

Even though I walk through the valley of the shadow of death, I will fear no evil, for you are with me; your rod and your staff, they comfort me.

O Mighty God,

Bless me as I use my God-given talent to create a gift for my dear friend. I pray Your
blessing on this special person You've allowed to come into my life. May Your gentle
touch reach out to this person I call a friend, someone I laugh with, cry with and pray
with. Bestow Your grace and goodness upon this person and enrich that person's life
as he or she has mine.

Amen.

Prayer for a Friend

Design by Diane Poellot

SKILL LEVEL

■■■□ INTERMEDIATE

FINISHED SIZE

22 x 69 inches

MATERIALS

• Patons Décor medium
(worsted) weight yarn
(3½ oz/210 yds/100g per ball):
8 balls #01619 softest country blue

- Size K/10½/6.5mm crochet hook or size needed to obtain gauge

GAUGE

2 diagonal shells = 3 inches; 1 diagonal shell row = 1 inch

SPECIAL STITCHES

Diagonal shell increase (diagonal shell inc): Ch 6, dc in 4th ch from hook, dc in each of next 2 chs.

Diagonal shell: (Sc, ch 2, 3 dc) in next ch sp.

Diagonal shell decrease (diagonal shell dec): Sl st in each of first 3 dc, (sl st, ch 3, 3 dc) in first ch sp.

INSTRUCTIONS

Row 1: Starting at bottom, **diagonal shell inc** *(see Special Stitches)*, turn. *(1 shell)*

Row 2: Diagonal shell inc, **diagonal shell** *(see Special Stitches)* in next ch sp, turn. *(2 shells)*

Row 3: Diagonal shell inc, shell in each ch sp across, turn. *(3 shells)*

Rows 4–29: Diagonal shell inc, shell in each ch sp across, turn. *(29 shells at end of last row)*

First Side

Row 30: Diagonal shell inc, shell in each of next 10 ch sps, sc in next ch sp, leaving rem ch sps unworked, turn. *(11 shells)*

Row 31: Diagonal shell dec *(see Special Stitches)*, shell in each ch sp across, turn.

Row 32: Diagonal shell inc, shell in each of next 10 ch sps, sc in last ch sp, turn.

Row 33: Diagonal shell dec, shell in each ch sp across, turn.

Row 34: Diagonal shell inc, shell in each of next 10 ch sps, sc in last ch sp, turn.

Row 35: Diagonal shell dec, shell in each ch sp across, turn.

Row 36: Diagonal shell inc, shell in each of next 10 ch sps, sc in last ch sp, turn.

Row 37: Diagonal shell dec, shell in each of next 9 ch sps, sc in last ch sp, turn.

Row 38: Diagonal shell dec, shell in each of next 8 ch sps, sc in last ch sp, turn.

Row 39: Diagonal shell dec, shell in each of next 7 ch sps, sc in last ch sp, turn.

Row 40: Diagonal shell dec, shell in each of next 6 ch sps, sc in last ch sp, turn.

Row 41: Diagonal shell dec, shell in each of next 5 ch sps, sc in last ch sp, turn.

Row 42: Diagonal shell dec, shell in each of next 4 ch sps, sc in last ch sp, turn.

Row 43: Diagonal shell dec, shell in each of next 3 ch sps, sc in last ch sp, turn.

Row 44: Diagonal shell dec, shell in each of next 2 ch sps, sc in last ch sp, turn.

Row 45: Diagonal shell dec, shell in next ch sp, sc in last ch sp, turn.

Row 46: Diagonal shell dec, sc in last ch sp, turn. Fasten off.

2nd Side

Row 30: Sk first 7 ch sps at top of row 29, join with sc in next ch sp, ch 2, 3 dc in same ch sp, shell in each ch sp across, turn. *(10 shells)*

Row 31: Diagonal shell inc, shell in each of next 10 ch sps, sc in last ch sp, turn.

Row 32: Diagonal shell dec, shell in each ch sp across, turn.

Row 33: Diagonal shell inc, shell in each of next 10 ch sps, sc in last ch sp, turn.

Row 34: Diagonal shell dec, shell in each ch sp across, turn.

Row 35: Diagonal shell inc, shell in each of next 10 ch sps, sc in last ch sp, turn.

Row 36: Diagonal shell dec, shell in each ch sp across, turn.

Row 37: Diagonal shell dec, shell in each of next 9 ch sps, sc in last ch sp, turn.

Row 38: Diagonal shell dec, shell in each of next 8 ch sps, sc in last ch sp, turn.

Row 39: Diagonal shell dec, shell in each of next 7 ch sps, sc in last ch sp, turn.

Row 40: Diagonal shell dec, shell in each of next 6 ch sps, sc in last ch sp, turn.

Row 41: Diagonal shell dec, shell in each of next 5 ch sps, sc in last ch sp, turn.

Row 42: Diagonal shell dec, shell in each of next 4 ch sps, sc in last ch sp, turn.

Row 43: Diagonal shell dec, shell in each of next 3 ch sps, sc in last ch sp, turn.

Row 44: Diagonal shell dec, shell in each of next 2 ch sps, sc in last ch sp, turn.

Row 45: Diagonal shell dec, shell in next ch sp, sc in last ch sp, turn.

Row 46: Diagonal shell dec, sc in last ch sp, turn.

Rnd 47: Now working in rounds around outer edge, 5 dc in center st or ch of next group, sl st in next ch sp or end of row, (2 dc, **fpdc**—*see Stitch Guide,* 2 dc) in center st or ch of next group, [sl st in next ch sp or end of row, 5 dc in center st or ch of next group, sl st in next ch sp or end of row, (2 dc, fpdc, 2 dc) in center st or ch of next group] around, join with sl st in last sc on row 46. Fasten off. •

Heavenly Father,

Bless my hands as they form this shawl of warmth and comfort. I recognize that You are our Father which art in Heaven, and I hallow your name. Please grant me patience, and help me to remember that You are aware of the trials and sufferings taking place in my life, in the lives of my friends and family and in the world. I recognize that You can turn anyone's trials and fears into blessings. Lord, give me peace of mind, peace of heart and peace of soul as I come to You and offer my thoughts, my words, my sufferings and the sufferings of the world around me. I pray that Your will be done, not mine. May I always remember that all things work to Your glory.

Amen.

Prayer for Peace

Design by Sandra Miller Maxfield

SKILL LEVEL

 ■■□□ EASY

FINISHED SIZE

39 x 51 inches

MATERIALS

• Lion Brand Homespun bulky (chunky) weight yarn 6 oz/185 yds/170g per skein):
   3 skeins #322 baroque
• Size K/10½/6.5mm crochet hook or size needed to obtain gauge

GAUGE

9 sts = 4 inches; rows 1–5 = 3¼ inches

PATTERN NOTES

Chain 2 at the beginning of row or round counts as first half double crochet unless otherwise stated.

Chain 5 at beginning of row or round counts as first treble crochet and chain 1 unless otherwise stated.

INSTRUCTIONS

Row 1: Ch 116, sc in 2nd ch from hook, [hdc in next ch, sc in next ch] across, turn. *(115 sts)*

Row 2: Ch 2 *(see Pattern Notes)*, [sc in next st, hdc in next st] across, turn.

Row 3: Ch 1, sc in first st, [hdc in next st, sc in next st] across, turn.

Row 4: Rep row 2.

Row 5: Ch 5 *(see Pattern Notes)*, sk next st, tr in next st, [ch 1, sk next st, tr in next st] across, turn.

Row 6: Ch 1, sc in first st, [hdc in next ch sp, sc in next st] across, turn.

Rows 7–61: [Rep rows 2–6 consecutively] 11 times.

Rows 62–64: Rep rows 2–4. At end of last row, fasten off. •

O Great Physician,

Give me compassion as I crochet this shawl. Help me to think of others first as You do. I pray that the recipient of this shawl will be healed and that You will send Your Holy Spirit to this person to surround him or her with Your presence in the recipient's time of need. Please reach Your strong, yet gentle, hands down to comfort the person and heal him or her broken sprit and body. Let him or her know that all things are possible through You. Be with the recipient in his or her moment of need for You are truly the Great Physician.

Amen.

Prayer for Healing

Design by Dorris Brooks

SKILL LEVEL

 EASY

FINISHED SIZE

47½ x 61½ inches, excluding Fringe

MATERIALS

 • Patons Décor medium (worsted) weight yarn (3½ oz/210 yds/100g per skein):

    6 skeins #01630 pale taupe

    3 skeins each #16605 burnt orange and #01633 chocolate taupe

• Size I/9/5.5mm crochet hook or size needed to obtain gauge

GAUGE

3 dc = 1 inch; 2 dc and 2 sc rows = 2 inches

PATTERN NOTE

Chain 3 at beginning of rows or rounds counts as first double crochet unless otherwise stated.

INSTRUCTIONS

Row 1: With burnt orange, ch 187, dc in 4th ch from hook *(first 3 chs count as first dc)*, dc in each ch across, turn. *(185 dc)*

Row 2: Ch 1, sc in each of first 2 sts, [tr in next st, sc in next st] across, ending with sc in last st, turn.

Row 3: Sc in each st across, turn.

Row 4: Rep row 2.

Row 5: Ch 3 *(see Pattern Note)*, dc in each st across, **do not turn.** Fasten off.

Row 6: Join pale taupe with sl st in first st, ch 3, dc in each st across, turn.

Rows 7–95: [Rep rows 2–6 consecutively] 18 times in color sequence of chocolate taupe, pale taupe and burnt orange, ending with row 5 and chocolate taupe. At end of last row, fasten off.

FRINGE

Cut 3 strands, each 15 inches long. Holding all strands tog, fold in half, pull fold through, pull ends through fold. Pull to tighten.

Matching colors, attach 3 Fringe evenly spaced across each color section on each short end. •

O Lord,

Almighty God, our heavenly Father, who ordained marriage to be a blessing, I thank You for family life, with all its joys and sorrows. Bless this hook as I crochet that it may become an instrument of Your love. As these two individuals join their lives together, may they know that You, the Creator, have brought them together as one. I ask that You will guide them into oneness of life as husband and wife, with each one looking at the other as chosen by God. Wrap them in your arms in times of unease and stress and give them the courage to say "I'm sorry" when they are wrong. May they always share hopes and dreams and look to You for comfort, strength and wisdom as they begin their lives together.
Amen.

Prayer for Love

Design by Deborah Levy-Hamburg

SKILL LEVEL

 EASY

FINISHED SIZE

40¾ x 48 inches, excluding Fringe

MATERIALS

• Medium (worsted) weight yarn:
35 oz/1,750 yds/992g white
• Size H/8/5mm crochet hook or size needed to obtain gauge

GAUGE

2 patterns = 6½ inches; 3 pattern rows = 2 inches

PATTERN NOTE

Chain 3 at the beginning of rows or rounds counts as first double crochet unless otherwise stated.

SPECIAL STITCH

Shell: 5 dc in next ch.

INSTRUCTIONS

Row 1: Ch 139, dc in 4th ch from hook *(first 3 chs count as first dc)*, dc in each of next 3 chs, [sk next 2 chs, **shell** *(see Special Stitch)* in next ch, ch 2, sk next 3 chs, dc in each of next 5 chs] across, turn. *(5 dc, 12 patterns)*

Rows 2–71: Ch 3 *(see Pattern Note)*, dc in each of next 4 sts, [sk next 2 chs, shell in next st, ch 2, sk next 4 sts, dc in each of next 5 sts] across, turn. At end of last row, fasten off.

FRINGE

Cut 16 strands, each 12 inches long. Holding all strands tog, fold in half. Pull fold through, pull ends through fold. Pull to tighten.

Attach 25 Fringe evenly spaced across each short end, beg and ending in corners. •

Dear God of Life,

I recognize that children truly are a gift from You, and I celebrate as You breathe life into this precious little being. May this child be blessed with good health in mind, body and spirit, and may this dear little one always have a loving heart. Lord, please help the parents to feel your calming presence and strength during the sometimes long and scary nights. Carry them through the late-night tiredness and help them to remember that this too will pass. I offer a prayer of thanks for this precious bundle made in Your image, and I ask that You send a band of angels for this child's protection, and I also pray for Your guidance to help both the mother and the father adapt to everything that will come with this tiny addition to the family.
Amen.

Prayer for a New Life

Design by Trudy Atteberry

SKILL LEVEL

 EASY

FINISHED SIZE

34 x 44½ inches

MATERIALS

 • Bernat Baby Coordinates light (light worsted) weight yarn (6 oz/431 yds/160g per skein):
   2 skeins #09612 daisy yellow
• Size K/10½/6.5mm crochet hook or size needed to obtain gauge

GAUGE

7 shells = 8 inches; 7 shell rows = 4 inches

SPECIAL STITCH

Shell: (2 dc, ch 2, sc) in next ch or ch sp.

INSTRUCTIONS

Row 1: Ch 119, shell *(see Special Stitch)* in 3rd ch from hook, [sk next 3 chs, shell in next ch] across, turn. *(30 shells)*

Rows 2–76: Ch 2, shell in each ch-2 sp across, turn. At end of last row, fasten off.

Row 77: Working in starting ch on opposite side of row 1, join with sc in first ch, (ch 2, 2 dc) in same ch, sk next 3 chs, [(sc, ch 2, 2 dc) in next ch, sk next 3 chs] across with (sc, ch 2, 2 dc, ch 2, sl st) in last ch. Fasten off. •

Lord God,

As I begin this shawl, clear my mind of clutter so that I may stay focused on the task
at hand. I pray that this shawl will act as Your loving arms wrapping the recipient
in a warm, calming embrace and gently reminding her of Your daily blessings and
continual love. Please send Your spirit to melt away all fears in this time of need
and grant the comfort and love that only comes from You.
Amen.

Prayer for a Loved One

Design by Elizabeth Ann White

SKILL LEVEL

■■□□ EASY

FINISHED SIZE

36 x 44 inches, excluding Fringe

MATERIALS

 • Bernat Berella "4" medium
(worsted) weight yarn
(3 oz/165 yds/85g per ball):
   4 balls #08973 terra cotta mist
• Size H/8/5mm crochet hook or size
   needed to obtain gauge

GAUGE

15 sc and chs = 4½ inches; 7 sc rows =
2 inches

INSTRUCTIONS

Row 1: Ch 130, sc in 2nd ch from
hook, [ch 1, sk next ch, sc in next ch]
across, turn. *(64 ch sps, 65 sc)*

Row 2: Ch 1, sc in first st, [ch 1, sk next
ch sp, sc in next st] across, turn.

Next rows: Rep row 2 until piece
measures 44 inches. At end of last row,
fasten off.

FRINGE

Cut 3 strands, each 12 inches long.
Holding all strands tog, fold in half,
pull fold through, pull ends through
fold. Pull to tighten.
Attach Fringe in each ch sp across row
1 and last row. •

Dear God,

Bless the shawl that my hands are about to create and make it a comfort and a blessing to the person who receives it. May she find peace during life's trials, setbacks, disappointments and hardships as she wraps herself in Your love and in this shawl. May it be a sign of Your loving presence and a reminder that she is surrounded by prayers asking You to give her wings to fly above her troubles. Amen.

Prayer for Comfort

Design by Tammie Godfrey

SKILL LEVEL

 INTERMEDIATE

FINISHED SIZE

38¾ inches long

MATERIALS

- Bernat Satin medium (worsted) weight yarn (3½ oz/163 yds/100g per ball): 4 balls #04011 sable
- Size G/6/4mm crochet hook or size needed to obtain gauge

GAUGE

3 dc groups and 2 ch sps = 3 inches; 3 dc rows = 2 inches

PATTERN NOTE

Chain 3 at the beginning of double crochet row or round counts as first double crochet unless otherwise stated.

INSTRUCTIONS

Row 1: Ch 6, sl st in first ch to form ring, ch 3 *(see Pattern Note)*, 2 dc in ring, ch 1, 3 dc in ring, turn. *(2 dc groups, 1 ch sp)*

Row 2: Ch 3, 2 dc in same st, ch 1, 3 dc in next ch sp, ch 1, sk next 2 dc, 3 dc in last st, turn. *(3 dc groups, 2 ch sps)*

Rows 3–55: Ch 3, 2 dc in same st, [3 dc, in next ch sp, ch 1] across to last 3 sts, sk next 2 sts, 3 dc in last st, turn. *(56 dc groups, 55 ch sps at end of last row)*

Row 56: Ch 3, 2 dc in same st, [3 dc in next ch sp, ch 1] across to last 3 sts, sk next 2 sts, 3 dc in last st, **do not turn.** *(57 dc groups, 56 ch sps)*

Edging

Working around outer edge, ch 1, 4 hdc in end of first row, [3 dc in end of next row, 4 hdc in end of next row] 27 times, 3 dc in end of next row, 4 hdc in ring, working on other side, [3 dc in end of next row, 4 hdc in end of next row] 28 times, working in sts and ch sps of last row, hdc in each of next 2 sts, [2 hdc in next ch sp, 2 hdc in next st, 3 dc in next st] 55 times, 2 hdc in last ch sp, hdc in each of last 2 sts, join with sl st in top of beg hdc. Fasten off. •

Dear God,

You are our hope and strength and a very present help in times of trouble. But, in the midst of pain and sorrow, You are often the last looked to for help. Please help this shawl to remind the one wearing it of Your love, giving this person a sense of peace because You are always with him or her.

Amen.

Prayer for Hope

Design by Elizabeth Ann White

SKILL LEVEL

 INTERMEDIATE

FINISHED SIZE

39 x 60 inches, including Border

MATERIALS

 • Caron Simply Soft medium (worsted) weight yarn
(6 oz/330 yds/170g per skein):

    2 skeins #9719 soft pink

    1 skein #9702 off white

• Size H/8/5mm crochet hook or size needed to obtain gauge

• ½-inch-wide ribbon: 2 yds pink

GAUGE

3 sc and 2 V-sts = 2½ inches; 5 pattern rows = 2½ inches

SPECIAL STITCHES

V-stitch (V-st): (Dc, ch 2, dc) in ch sp as indicated.

Double love knot: [Pull up 1-inch long lp on hook *(see Fig. 1)*, yo, pull through lp, sc in back strand of long lp] twice.

Love knot: Pull up 1-inch long lp on hook *(see Fig. 1)*, yo, pull through lp, sc in back strand of long lp.

Figure 1

Step 1:

Step 2:

Completed Love Knot

Step 3:

INSTRUCTIONS

Row 1: With soft pink, ch 124, sc in 2nd ch from hook, sk next ch, **V-st** *(see Special Stitches)* in next ch, [sk next ch, sc in next ch, sk next ch, V-st in next ch] across, turn. *(31 sc, 31 V-sts)*

Rows 2–107: Ch 1, sc in ch sp of first V-st, V-st in next sc, [sc in ch sp of next V-st, V-st in next sc] across, turn. At end of last row, fasten off.

Border

Rnd 1: Working in ends of rows, in sc and in ch sps of V-sts, join off white with sl st in end of first row, (ch 5, dc) in same row *(corner)*, ch 1, [dc in next end of next row, ch 1] across to next corner,

(dc, ch 2, dc) in corner, ch 1, [dc in next sc or ch sp of next V-st, ch 1] across to next corner, (dc, ch 2, dc) in corner, ch 1, [dc in next end of next row, ch 1] across to next corner, (dc, ch 2, dc) in corner, ch 1, working in starting ch on opposite side of row 1, [dc in next worked ch, ch 1] across, join with sl st in 3rd ch of beg ch-3.

Rnd 2: (Sl st, sc, **double love knot**—*see Special Stitches*, sc) in first corner ch sp, (sc, double love knot) in each ch sp around with (sc, double love knot, sc) in each corner ch sp, join with sl st in beg sc.

Rnds 3 & 4: Love knot (*see Special Stitches*), (sc, double love knot, sc) in center of first double love knot of first corner, double love knot, [sc in center

of next double love knot, double love knot] around with (sc, double love knot, sc) in center of each double love knot of each corner, join with sl st in beg sc. At end of last rnd, fasten off.

BOWS

Cut ribbon into 4 pieces, each 18 inches long. Tie each piece in Bow around 1 st at each corner of rnd 1 of Border. •

Stitch Guide

Abbreviations

beg	begin/beginning
bpdc	back post double crochet
bpsc	back post single crochet
bptr	back post treble crochet
CC	contrasting color
ch	chain stitch
ch-	refers to chain or space previously made (i.e., ch-1 space)
ch sp	chain space
cl	cluster
cm	centimeter(s)
dc	double crochet
dec	decrease/decreases/decreasing
dtr	double treble crochet
fpdc	front post double crochet
fpsc	front post single crochet
fptr	front post treble crochet
g	gram(s)
hdc	half double crochet
inc	increase/increases/increasing
lp(s)	loop(s)
MC	main color
mm	millimeter(s)
oz	ounce(s)
pc	popcorn
rem	remain/remaining
rep	repeat(s)
rnd(s)	round(s)
RS	right side
sc	single crochet
sk	skip(ped)
sl st	slip stitch
sp(s)	space(s)
st(s)	stitch(es)
tog	together
tr	treble crochet
trtr	triple treble crochet
WS	wrong side
yd(s)	yard(s)
yo	yarn over

Chain—ch: Yo, pull through lp on hook.

Slip stitch—sl st: Insert hook in st, pull through Both lps on hook.

Single crochet—sc: Insert hook in st, yo, pull through st, yo, pull through both lps on hook.

Front post stitch—fp: Back post stitch—bp: When working post st, insert hook from right to left around post st on previous row.

Front loop—front lp Back loop— back lp

Front Loop   Back Loop

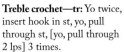

Half double crochet—hdc: Yo, insert hook in st, yo, pull through st, yo, pull through all 3 lps on hook.

Double crochet—dc: Yo, insert hook in st, yo, pull through st, [yo, pull through 2 lps] twice.

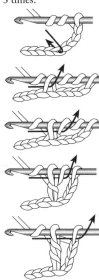

Change colors: Drop first color; with 2nd color, pull through last 2 lps of st.

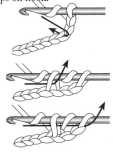

Treble crochet—tr: Yo twice, insert hook in st, yo, pull through st, [yo, pull through 2 lps] 3 times.

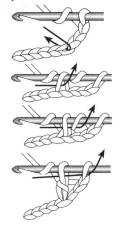

Double treble crochet—dtr: Yo 3 times, insert hook in st, yo, pull through st, [yo, pull through 2 lps], 4 times.

Single crochet decrease (sc dec): (Insert hook, yo, draw lp through) in each of the sts indicated, yo, draw through all lps on hook.

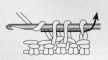

Example of 2-sc dec

Half double crochet decrease (hdc dec): (Yo, insert hook, yo, draw lp through) in each of the sts indicated, yo, draw through all lps on hook.

Example of 2-hdc dec

Double crochet decrease (dc dec): (Yo, insert hook, yo, draw loop through, draw through 2 lps on hook) in each of the sts indicated, yo, draw through all lps on hook.

Example of 2-dc dec

Example of 2-tr dec

Treble crochet decrease (tr dec): Holding back last lp of each st, tr in each of the sts indicated, yo, pull through all lps on hook.

US		UK
sl st (slip stitch)	=	sc (single crochet)
sc (single crochet)	=	dc (double crochet)
hdc (half double crochet)	=	htr (half treble crochet)
dc (double crochet)	=	tr (treble crochet)
tr (treble crochet)	=	dtr (double treble crochet)
dtr (double treble crochet)	=	ttr (triple treble crochet)
skip	=	miss

Gift Tags

May a house of love always be yours.
Congratulations on your wedding!

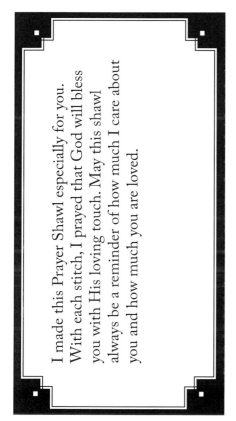

I made this Prayer Shawl especially for you. With each stitch, I prayed that God will bless you with His loving touch. May this shawl always be a reminder of how much I care about you and how much you are loved.

I can do all things through Christ which strengthened me.
Philippians 4:13

A hundred years from now
it will not matter what kind of car you drove,
Or what kind of house you lived in,
But the world may be a better place
because you were important,
In the life of a child.
— Unknown
Congratulations on your new arrival!

Annie's Attic®

Copyright ©2007 DRG 306 East Parr Road, Berne, IN 46711. All rights reserved.
This publication may not be reproduced in part or in whole without written permission from the publisher.

TOLL-FREE ORDER LINE or to request a free catalog (800) LV-ANNIE (800) 582-6643
Customer Service (800) AT-ANNIE (800) 282-6643, **Fax** (800) 882-6643
Visit anniesattic.com

We have made every effort to ensure the accuracy and completeness of these instructions.
We cannot, however, be responsible for human error, typographical mistakes or variations in individual work.

ISBN: 978-1-59635-178-3

Printed in USA   5 6 7 8 9 10 11 12 13 14 15